Books by Michael McGriff

Poetry
Early Hour
Black Postcards
Home Burial
Dismantling the Hills

Fiction
Our Secret Life in the Movies (with J.M. Tyree)

Translation
The Sorrow Gondola, by Tomas Tranströmer (translated with
Mikaela Grassl)

As Editor
To Build My Shadow a Fire: The Poetry and Translations of David Wevill

Michael McGriff
Early Hour

COPPER CANYON PRESS

PORT TOWNSEND, WASHINGTON

Cover art: Clive Collie / Alamy Stock Photo

Copper Canyon Press is in residence at Fort Worden State Park in Port Townsend, Washington, under the auspices of Centrum. Centrum is a gathering place for artists and creative thinkers from around the world, students of all ages and backgrounds, and audiences seeking extraordinary cultural enrichment.

LIBRARY OF CONGRESS CATALOGING-IN-PUBLICATION DATA

Names: McGriff, Michael, 1976–, author.
Title: Early hour / Michael McGriff.
Description: Port Townsend, WA : Copper Canyon Press, [2017]
Identifiers: LCCN 2016058848 (print) | LCCN 2017005105 (ebook)
  | ISBN 9781556595073 (paperback) | ISBN 9781619321748 (E-book)
Subjects: | BISAC: POETRY / American / General.
Classification: LCC PS3613.C4973 A6 2017 (print) | LCC PS3613.C4973 (ebook)
  | DDC 811/.6—dc23
LC record available at https://lccn.loc.gov/2016058848

98765432 first printing

Copper Canyon Press
Post Office Box 271
Port Townsend, Washington 98368
www.coppercanyonpress.org

for Margot

Contents

Early Hour

Early Hour

In the early hour.
In the hour of copper.
In the secret minutes
coiled around wooden spools
and scrawled into the sill dust
beneath our open window.
In this room lit up
like the throatlatch
of a horse, like sea-foam
under the breeze of a black moon.
You are asleep, the dog
collapsed between us,
the shadows across your stomach
umber-flecked and swimming
toward some vague memory of blue
that the early hour
has wrung from its hair.
Your breath smells of farriers' hammers,
of April spreading its sheer fabric
among the first blooms
of the dogwoods.
The edge of the floodplain
is a red crescent
and you shimmer
like an ax-head lost in the creek.
When the whereabouts
of the azaleas

become uncertain,
the outline of your face
is sky-written in the black loam
of the thunderheads.
When Cygnus scrapes his iron beak
against the rafters,
when the cathedrals
in each whitecap
cross the river,
when the dog's skull
fills with green light
and a bucket of sparks
empties onto the mantle-dark
shoulders of this early hour,
you become the early hour.
You become water
dressing up as the opposite
of bone and rags,
you become an island
filling with reeds,
the shore wind repeating itself,
the sound of two feathers
crossing one over the other
among threads of dust.
You sail past the dead
with their saffron-yellow teeth,
their gristmill jaws,
and their wings clipped back
to callused nubs.

In this early hour
I hear a rustling
in the dogwoods,
the sound of a table
being set, a deck of cards
sliding across the crushed lip
of its box.
I hear the rail yard
draw an arrow
to the edge of our country—
and though there are no trains,
a few dogs run mad beside them
through the tall,
impossibly blue grass
as you drift within your body
and into an hour as nameless
as the stone heart of a plum.

Why I Am Obsessed with Horses

Because when I saw a horse
cross a river
separating two countries
it said *My name is 1935*
because it also spoke in tongues
as it crossed the black tongue
of the water
because it still arcs through me
with its zodiac
of shrapnel-bright stars
because the river's teeth
still gnash
against its flank
and its eyes
still have the luster
of black china
glowing black-bright
in the glass hutch of memory
because a horse's skull
is a ditch of wildflowers
because a horse's skull
is a box of numbers
a slop bucket
resting upside down
under barn eaves
wind in an empty stockyard
orange clay that breaks

shovel handles
because a horse is the underwriter
of all motion
because a horse is the first
and last item
on every list
of every season
and because that night the air
smelled green as copper
and lath dust
and that night as it scrambled
up the bank and stamped past me
it said *I am the source of all echoes.*

Black Postcard

In bed, I smoke my last cigarette.
You are attached
to a cable of moonlight.
Your chest rises and falls
and my thoughts fall like ribbons
through the branches
as the sound of a crow
scissors past the window.
We are black postcards
smuggled into the early hour
under its wing.

Inventory

We've driven beyond the night
with its burning headdress
of pulleys and frayed rope,
beyond the smell of shale
and saddle oil,
beyond the sandstone dreaming
its cadmium dream
and the broken teeth
and false friends
penciling themselves into my days,
the humming cables
and diesel fumes,
the light from a thigh-high stocking
filled with unmatched spoons,
and the slate-dark hem
of the county line.
We've driven beyond
last summer's dead crows wired
by their feet to these fence posts,
beyond the sheet ice
with its death-tongue crawling up
from the jeweled throat
of the river.
We've driven beyond the night
into the new year,
and I've thrown your leg across me
and you're giving me

the torque and tremor
of your animal waist
and I'm wearing your pinion hips
like a crown of kerosene
and I'm grabbing your hair
like a fistful of raffle tickets
and you're exploding over me
like river rocks
in the horizon's mouth
and your body glows
like an open boxcar
punched through
with light the color
of the high-water mark
stained across the moon.

Flat Light

This hour and its blue wave
slip from their world to ours
beneath the camber
of your foot.

The snow across the fields
in its all-at-once-here-all-at-once-gone,
the light stretched flat
and dreamless,
and the power lines
touching their foreheads
to the ground.

The Afterlife

Even here, the stars are lug nuts
lost in the saw grass
and my boots disappear
into the soft shoulder
of the ditch.
I forget my hometown
and my country forgets my name.
Somehow, my life is reduced
to the lies I cut free
from the newspaper.
I start a fire with them
and sleep next to it
with a woman
who's lit from within
like jasper underwater,
like quail eggs
and suicide knobs.

Degenerate

It's true, I'm full
of dead lawn chairs
and wet parking lots,
lottery tickets and gray fires
burning at the edges
of small towns.
I'm a wild donkey dusted
in frozen rain.
I'm dumb as a cistern.
I'm the wrong mix
of air and gasoline,
a piano stored in a barn.
I hear the snow fences
near Powder Creek
trying to draw my grave
on December's maps.
But I've pressed my ear
to the hive of your back
with its blue vapors
and lost tribes.
I've listened to the owls
coursing inside you.
I've held the night's wrist
against my face,
trying to get back
to the signal fires
of your hips.

I'm on the edge of the pier
waiting for you
to pour hot oil
through every machine in me.

Black Postcard

The runoff creek
and its threads of blue light
want to outlive everything here,

even the spur gears
running their black orbits
through the oil bath
in a horse's skull.

I listen to something stamp
across the night's blank face.

Cosmology

The river moves
beneath the sheet ice.
The wind is a grand hall
of records.
In the recipe box
above the refrigerator,
the deathbed photos
of four generations—
somewhere, their hands
have turned to prime numbers.
Somewhere, a voice
that smells like a well bucket
rearranges the vowels
of my name.
Woman of wet rope
and cordwood,
woman with pant cuffs
of smoke, I feel myself
spinning back to rest
within a singular
shade of carbon.

Your Name Is a Country

Under the blood-drunk moon,
under Corvus
and his cup of thirst,
the clock strikes the same hour
every hour

and the river is lit
by the gaslight of fish eyes
and warmed by the straw fire
inside the shale.

I hear a crow's tongue
translating *darkness*
into *asp* and *cone file*.

I hear the chrome plant
unspool itself
upstream
in a ceremony
of cobalts and pewters,

but what I hear most
is your name
undressing
and whistling
through the early hour's
wooden teeth,

your name
with its mouthful of door keys,
those two syllables
like two mantles
in a gas lantern swinging
like two bells
tied to the neck of a horse.

If your name
is rewound to its source,
to the hinge of this moment,
and if this moment
vanishes like the horse
whose chest disappears
beneath the water
during a river crossing,
and if the wind sleeps
in the horse's downstream ear,
and if the river is a turkey feather
slid between your name
and the moon,
then your name
is a country.

Relatives of the Dead

The dead man's suit coat
is a good fit through the shoulders.

The last thing he touched
is the first thing I touch,
the silky floral lining inside
the left sleeve.

Spools of black thread unravel
over the graves of close friends.

Sleeping beside White River

The moon is fishing for compliments
along the sandbar, and I'm holding
a banquet for our separateness,
a white table runner unfolding
forever out and away.
The river and its mineral echoes.
Gravel roads like an idea for the map
of a drunk's broken hand.
Ferns in their gowns of dust
and the glaciers off to the west
telling their usual lies about beauty.
Rat in the ditch of my heart gnawing
at a plastic bag, your crown
of long vowels tilted to one side,
certain and with music.

The Afterlife

Even here, it's the same trick.
As you wade into Coffin Creek
the trout hide in the snag-shadows
and the bloom of glitter-silt
clouding your ankles
is just me throwing my voice.

Black Postcard

In my dream
a farm is requisitioned
and I fall through myself
one color at a time,
the way a crow
wired to a fence by its feet
watches itself
fall through itself
with the black milk
of its own eye.
I gather twigs, straw, and mud.
Wings grow from my back
and sound like a field
wearing a hatch
of new flies.

Letter Sewn into the Hem of a Dress
Made of Smoke

I wake beside you,
blood sloshing
in my skull's chipped saucer,
the stars trolling overhead,
and a dirt road
that twists back
to its own prehistory.

When I say you have the beauty
of a dirt road
I mean you have thin shoulders
that twist in me
like the fault lines
in a minor planet's moon.

I mean you smell of dust,
burnt soapstone, beetle shells,
a garden hose limp in the sun.

I can feel you
tilt your head back
and tell some fleck of dust
hanging between us
that you make noises
only the dog can hear.

I've lived all these years
with my mouth
pressed to the altar
of low green rivers
and slabs of shale,
and I'm telling you now
I can feel the night
scrawling the shape
of your voice
onto the cold wet earth.

And when I say a doe
is about to jump
the low spot in the fence
in December
in the rain
in this moment
and no other, I mean
your animal stillness
resting next to mine.

Communiqué

We've been told
it's worse in every direction,
that it's safest to stay
exactly where we are.

We've been told
it's best to divorce ourselves
from the old system
and adopt the new system.

Handbills fall from the sky
with instructions
to seal off the windows and doors.

The dishes shake
in the cupboards.
The hills, mute as fish,
appear to glow.

I hear vines
growing up through the lake.
They reach for the moon
like the hair of the dead.

Skipping a Funeral

I sit near the kitchen window
and remember a lie I forgot to tell him.
Steam hangs over the crossties
in the garden. I'm reading,
but not really reading,
a book written in coal smoke,
its forced marches and the systematic
extermination of language.
Soon, I will be the barn-dark space
between the trees.

Highway 67

The night sky
and its pageants of ink
its barrel fires
its immigrant stowaways
its stars like silverware drawers
emptied into some hallway
of memory
its desire to light up
the ears of the mule
the way it ties
our wrists together
with baling wire
the wick of it
its deep-dark prow
the hum of its gearbox
its salt
the whale bones
it drags through the meridian
the way it dreams
the dreams of dreams
the way I swell
like a cedar plank
when the night sky opens
its canning jars of smoke
and I press my tongue
to the wet rope
of a vein
in your neck.

Black Postcard

The mineral shadow rising
from the ruined mouth of the city
drifts across the blood moon.
The bones of the dogwoods
stained yellow as the teeth of widows
scrape against the distance
between our bed and the muted hills.
There are certain corpses
whose eyes never close,
whose jewels are pried loose
and arranged
across the meridian.

Drinking at Roger's Bar

The bones in a possum's hand
are a set of reduction gears
turning in a machine that brings light
to this valley of burnt oil
and narrow rivers
where my favorite drunks,
a few chairs down, laugh hard,
forming a theory of everything.

Equinox

As we lie here, the peacocks
throw down their cries
of oiled ribbon and hot wax
through the hydraulic night

while Ursa Major
loops your name
across one black postcard
after another.

The rhododendrons
speak in tongues.
The sea loses count
of its dead.

Along the ridge of your body,
the music of trace chains,
the light of the plough.

The alders raise their masts
and hammer out
their ancient telegrams.

On the floor,
in my shirt pocket,
eight metric bolts
calling out
to some lost machine.

With Delmore

With a few slits
and a hard yank,
he "prom dressed"
the brush rabbit
then tossed its pelt
to the river.

"Just because it looks like an eye,"
he would say of the moon,
"don't mean it can see shit."

He smelled like a gopher snake
in a dry woodshed.
He drank coffee the color
of grasshopper spit.
He had the face of a shad
and thin wrists.

"I've seen things
and I know things,"
he said, as the pelt spun
into the black spikes
of an eddy, as the sky
opened its mouth
over the hills
and struck a match
on its dry tooth.

Black Postcard

Before you undressed,
a thread lowered itself
from the cuff of your sleeve
and drank at the trees
quivering upside down
in your cup.

Overlook, Cape Arago

These waters ask permission of nothing,
and I've placed my thoughts for you
in a nest of copper shavings.

December tries on its glittering outfits
over the mirrors of our bodies.

At the end of the long hallway of your voice
is a room with a globe
where the sounds of green rivers
and the names of small towns
share their secrets in the late, dusty light.

I've translated your name into the languages
of salt—I've sent each one out on a small raft
across the ink-dark thorns grinding in the sea.

Between the cargo nets of your throat and my mouth
is something that will outlast the dark.

The Afterlife

Even here, the cows
look like diesel engines
hardly worth repairing

and the Ferris wheel's gondola
lies buried on its side
in the hayfield
near the chrome plant

and you're flat
on your stomach,
hands bound,
the horse in front of you
stamping in place,
ready to drag you
for eternity
as soon as I drop
this red kerchief
from my iron fist.

If You Are Water

Tonight, the whiskey fires
burning on the moon
move through me like a hammer
swung in the dark,
and if you are water the moon
is painting itself across you.
If you are water I am running my hands
through you. If you are water
my left hand is a horse thief
and my right hand is alder smoke
drifting the ridge.
I am the old dike road
and you are pushing your wet shoulders
into the black silt of me.
I am a piece of glass
falling through itself.
But you are not water
and I am on my knees bent over the edge
of the dock, moving my hands
through the vague glimmer
of distant cities, the bioluminescence
coiled around each finger.

New Year

After four winters,
rail service has returned to town.
The wind paints new,
suicidal minutes
onto the face of the clock
over the boathouse.

The grass is defiant,
wild, frost-brined,
and reluctant
to take any shape—
it also carries the sound
of the wind,
which has just lain down
in the grave of my hands.

Opening Gambit

Two decommissioned highways cross
toward their borders
with the casual certainty
the dead carry in their sample cases.
Leaning against the wind
I notice tufts of fur in the air
and a driveshaft rising from the sand,
then the horsehair of a violinist's bow
drawn steadily across my neck.

Walking the Property Line

There is a barn full of light
building itself inside me.
Rafters, floor joists,
the old plank flooring,
everything touched
by the kind of light
I always knew existed
but never knew the name of.
The light carries the sound
of wild turkeys scurrying
the barbed-wire fence
near the one Stop sign
for eight miles.
The sound of the tide
on its dark stilts.
The sound of winter's runoff creeks
and gray-throated rocks.
I have set a table. It is simple.
I am waiting for you there.
When I see you,
I will kiss the top of your head
the way a saint kisses
the feet of a stranger.
I will light you on fire
and carry you into the night.

Near Dingle Creek

According to certain parameters,
I'm standing in the most remote point
in my country, and my left hand rests
on the long ellipse of the evening.

Other parameters have not been met,
and my life feels like a shop rag
stuffed into a wasp's nest,
diesel-soaked and alight,
a whimper trickling through
an endless field of the canyon's dusty ear.

I scrape at a truck's corroded battery terminals
with a screwdriver, and a small pile of bones
makes a nest in my shadow.
I'm standing on the old seafloor
where owls live in burrows
among roots and smoke
harvested from the red clay.

Cosmology for the New Year

The light from dead stars only exists
in the minds of the living,
and at night the salt-echoes of your hips
fall through me like a lost set of keys.

In the moment between
the end of one longing
and the beginning of another
I hear the boundary waters
of this century in your hair
and cross them by horse.

Black Postcard

I press my ear to your back.
In the floodplain
one brittle reed is played
with a breath that starts somewhere
beneath the earth.
I hear two slender
beautifully veined feet
stepping out onto the high-wire
of your voice.

I Am an Ox in the Year of the Horse

Your hands have made a yoke
a bright chain of grinding stars
around my neck
and you are pulling me into you
and you have turned me into an ox
of mineral fires and sweat
and you are working me
and I can't tell whether I'm falling inside you
or climbing the mantled dark of you
but I can feel myself moving
through the origin of numbers and carbon
and I can feel your ankles lock around my back
and they too are giving their orders
but they are also two thrushes
volleying their cries against
the invisible canyon of basalt
and you are working me
and I have reached some place in you
where I gnaw down the doors in you
and my teeth grow numb as drunk fishermen
and all the roots in you
suck the water from me
and I enter a depth in you
that pulls your name from my throat
and you are working me
and I'm telling you I am your pilgrim
your animal your thief your pyre

your anvil and echo
and I want to be bound and burned here
and collapse here and beg here and pound here
and unspool one long sound from my body
into this kingdom
where we are two wet shades of black
swimming into the first evening of the universe.

Acknowledgments

Academy of American Poets: Poem-a-Day "Opening Gambit," "Why I Am Obsessed with Horses"

Alaska Quarterly Review: "Degenerate"

The American Poetry Review: "Cosmology," "Equinox," "Skipping a Funeral," "Sleeping beside White River"

The Believer: "Drinking at Roger's Bar"

Jai-Alai Magazine: "Black Postcard [In bed, I smoke my last cigarette]," "Black Postcard [In my dream]"

Narrative: "Cosmology for the New Year," "Highway 67," "If You Are Water," "New Year," "Overlook, Cape Arago," "Relatives of the Dead," "With Delmore"

Poetry London: "Inventory"

Poetry Northwest: "The Afterlife [Even here, the stars are lug nuts]," "Early Hour," "Letter Sewn into the Hem of a Dress Made of Smoke"

Tin House: "I Am an Ox in the Year of the Horse," "Walking the Property Line"

"Early Hour," "Inventory," "Sleeping beside White River," and "Your Name Is a Country" appear in the chapbook *Black Postcards* as part of the Acme Poem Company Surrealist Poetry Series (Willow Springs Books, 2017).

"Communiqué" appears in the short story collection *Our Secret Life in the Movies,* coauthored with J.M. Tyree (A Strange Object, 2014).

Lines and images from various poems appear in an untitled poem in the photography collection *Islands of the Blest* edited by Bryan Schutmaat and Ashlyn Davis (The Silas Finch Foundation, 2014).

For institutional support, editorial advice, and friendship, the author thanks James Magnuson, Marla Akin, and Debbie Dewees at the James A. Michener Center for Writers; Alexandra Teague and Robert Wrigley at the University of Idaho; Matthew O'Malley, Kate Lebo, Malachi Black, Andrew Grace, Robert Hunter Jones, David Wevill, J.M. Tyree, Matthew Dickman, Michael Dickman, Joseph Millar, Dorianne Laux, and Margot Volem.

Notes

"Early Hour": *Frühe Stunde* (*Early Hour*), Karl Hofer (German, 1878–1955), 1935, oil on canvas, 49¼ × 61⅜ inches.

The "Black Postcard" poems borrow their titles from a poem by Tomas Tranströmer and are dedicated to his memory.

"Sleeping beside White River" is for Frosty Davis.

About the Author

Michael McGriff is an author, editor, and translator. His recent books include the story collection *Our Secret Life in the Movies* (coauthored with J.M. Tyree), one of NPR's Best Books of 2014, and the poetry collection *Home Burial*, a *New York Times Book Review* Editors' Choice. His work has appeared in *The American Poetry Review, The Believer,* the *New York Times, Poetry London, Tin House,* and on PBS's *NewsHour*. His honors include a Lannan Literary Fellowship, a Stegner Fellowship, and a grant from the National Endowment for the Arts. He is a member of the creative writing faculty at the University of Idaho.

Poetry is vital to language and living. Since 1972, Copper Canyon Press has published extraordinary poetry from around the world to engage the imaginations and intellects of readers, writers, booksellers, librarians, teachers, students, and donors.

WE ARE GRATEFUL FOR THE MAJOR SUPPORT PROVIDED BY:

THE PAUL G. ALLEN
FAMILY FOUNDATION

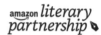

TO LEARN MORE ABOUT UNDERWRITING
COPPER CANYON PRESS TITLES,
PLEASE CALL 360-385-4925 EXT. 103

WE ARE GRATEFUL FOR THE MAJOR SUPPORT PROVIDED BY:

Anonymous

Jill Baker and Jeffrey Bishop

Donna and Matt Bellew

John Branch

Diana Broze

Sarah and Tim Cavanaugh

Janet and Les Cox

Catherine Eaton and David Skinner

Mimi Gardner Gates

Linda Gerrard and Walter Parsons

Gull Industries, Inc.
   on behalf of William and
   Ruth True

The Trust of Warren A. Gummow

Steven Myron Holl

Lakeside Industries, Inc.
   on behalf of Jeanne Marie Lee

Maureen Lee and Mark Busto

Rhoady Lee and Alan Gartenhaus

Ellie Mathews and Carl Youngmann
   as The North Press

Anne O'Donnell and John Phillips

Petunia Charitable Fund
   and advisor Elizabeth Hebert

Suzie Rapp and Mark Hamilton

Joseph C. Roberts

Jill and Bill Ruckelshaus

Cynthia Lovelace Sears and
   Frank Buxton

Kim and Jeff Seely

Dan Waggoner

Austin Walters

Barbara and Charles Wright

The dedicated interns and
   faithful volunteers of
   Copper Canyon Press

The Chinese character for poetry is made up of two parts:
"word" and "temple." It also serves as pressmark for
Copper Canyon Press.

The poems are set in Fournier. Headings are set in Futura.
Printed on archival-quality paper.
Book design and composition by Phil Kovacevich.